779

KT-489-134

American Photography Three

EDITED BY EDWARD BOOTH-CLIBBORN

American Photography Three

*The third annual of
American editorial, advertising
and poster, book, promotion and
unpublished photography*

Booth-Clibborn Editions

Donna Vinciguerra *Project Director*
Fred Woodward, Jolene Cuyler *Designers*
Rosalie Winard *Assistant Editor*
Diana Darling *Design Assistant*
Annie Leibovitz *Jacket photograph*
Jim Myers *Title page photographs*

Captions and artwork in this book have
been supplied by the entrants. While every
effort has been made to ensure accuracy,
American Photography Inc. does not under
any circumstances accept any
responsibility for errors or omissions.

If you are a practicing photographer or
student and would like to submit work to
the next annual competition, the deadline
each year will be November 10. For more
information write to:
American Photography Inc.
67 Irving Place
New York, NY 10003
(212) 460-5558

Copyright © 1987 Call For Entries
American Photography Inc.

Distributed in the United States and Canada:
Harry N. Abrams Inc.
100 Fifth Avenue
New York, NY 10011
ISBN 0-8109-1860-9

Distributed in the United Kingdom:
Internos Books
Colville Road
London W3 8BL, England
ISBN 0-904866-53-X

© 1987, Sté N^{lle} des Éditions du Chêne, Paris
pour l'édition en langue française
ISBN: 2.85108.530.1
Dépôt légal: n° 5184-octobre 1987
34/0691/5

Book trade inquiries for the rest of the world:
Hearst Books International
105 Madison Avenue
New York, NY 10016, USA

Direct mail for the world:
Internos Books
Colville Road
London W3 8BL, England

Direct mail for U.S.A. and Canada:
Print Books
6400 Goldsboro Road
Bethesda, MD 20817

Published by Booth-Clibborn

Printed and bound in Japan by Dai Nippon
Paper: 157 GSM Coated
Display type: Corvinus Skyline
Text type: News Gothic Bold Extended, Baskerville
Typesetting: Type Foundry, Phil's Photo, Inc.
Washington, D.C.

Copyright © 1987
by Polygon Editions S.A.R.L. Basel

Plates 129 and 130:
Copyright © by Joel-Peter Witkin
Courtesy Pace/MacGill Gallery, New York/
Fraenkel Gallery, San Francisco

Contents

Photograph by BRIAN SMALE

Introduction

by Edward Booth-Clibborn

"Bang, bang, you're dead."

It takes just a moment for a child to shoot his best friend, just as it takes only a moment to make a photograph.

Looking through this book you'll find some captured moments of exquisite poignancy, some of stark drama, and some of simple beauty. I hope that if you're a budding professional or an enthusiastic amateur, these captured ·moments will encourage you—even inspire you—for they show that, for the photographer, all life is a subject.

Of course, many of the photographs here are not those windows on the world. Indeed, much of the work here was conceived by an art director and executed by a photographer, both of them working to a brief.

Yet here again is food for thought.

On the one hand the camera is used to distill an essence of life; on the other it is used to create an image—of wealth, glamour, danger, fear, joy, or whatever the subject calls for.

What runs through all the work is the quality we always look for in choosing work for these annuals: excellence. Whether the camera is used as a paint box or a propagandist's tool, we are concerned with the highest standards of thought, observation, imagination, composition, and execution. As such, this is a rare book. To have your work included in it is a rare achievement. This year there are many new names for the index, many new photographers whose belief in their work and love of their craft is the driving force behind their success.

I hope you enjoy the work, and that you'll want to submit your own images to American Photography, whether they be captured moments or more contrived ideas.

As the man said, "You've got to be in to win." And if you're not? Well, as the boy said, "Bang, bang..."

The Jury

Walter Bernard, Peter Howe,

Laurie Kratochvil, Fred Woodward,

Jack Woody

Walter Bernard

Photograph by WILLIAM COUPON

Walter Bernard was assistant art director of Esquire magazine until 1968 when he moved to New York magazine to be its art director. In 1977, he was named art director of Time magazine; he redesigned Time. In the next few years he redesigned such magazines as Adweek, Atlantic Monthly and Fortune. He was design director of Fortune until 1983 when he left to form WBMG, Inc., an editorial and development firm, with Milton Glaser. Walter Bernard is a member of the board of directors of the American Institute of Graphic Arts.

Peter Howe

Photograph by DAVID BURNETT

Peter Howe developed an interest in photography while working for his bachelor's degree in fine arts at the University of Newcastle Upon Tyne. He served as assistant to two photographers in London started his career in photojournalism working for the BBC and for such publications as the London Sunday Times Magazine, The Observer Magazine and Nova. He came to the United States in 1979 as a photographer for The Observer and for Bipa, a French press agency. Married to New York Daily News journalist Anthea Disney, Peter is photo editor of The New York Times Magazine.

Photograph by DEBORAH FEINGOLD

Laurie Kratochvil joined Rolling Stone as photography editor in 1979 after working at the Los Angeles Times and A&M Records. She left Rolling Stone to work as photography editor at New West (renamed California) magazine and served as a consultant for Warner Bros. Pictures, Condé Nast and several design firms. In 1982 she returned to Rolling Stone as the photography editor, the title she currently holds.

Fred Woodward

Photograph by MATT MAHURIN

Fred Woodward is currently working on a redesign of Regardie's magazine in Washington, D.C. As the Art Director of Texas Monthly, Westward and D Magazine, his work was featured in all the major graphic design publications and won numerous awards, including gold medals from the Society of Publication Designers. He has been taking photographs for the last five years.

Jack Woody

Photograph by HERB RITTS

Saw his first memorable photograph at age six; a movie still of grandmother Helen Twelvetrees on her knees in a church doorway, crying in her wedding dress. Thought this had something to do with her subsequent real-life divorce. Later learned the difference between the facts of the photograph and the facts of life. Understood around the age of ten that a good lie is the art of the commercial photographer and a photograph is only as interesting as the man or woman behind it. At 23, founded Twelvetrees Press, which publishes artists who print, draw and use a camera.

Editorial

*Photographs for
newspaper supplements;
consumer, trade
and technical magazines
and periodicals*

plate

1

April Silver *Art Director*
Ellen Madere *Picture Editor*
Esquire *Publication*
James Kaplan *Writer*
Hearst Corporation *Publisher*

To make the definitive photo for "Who is David Byrne? What is David Byrne?
Does David Byrne matter?" George Hurrell went to Texas where Byrne was working on
the movie "True Stories." January 1986.

plate

2

plate
3

Derek Ungless *Art Director*
Laurie Kratochvil *Picture Editor*
Rolling Stone *Publication*
Charles Leerhsen *Writer*
Straight Arrow Publishers Inc. *Publisher*

*"Do You Believe in Magic?" asked Charles Leerhsen's article on the magicians
Penn and Teller. December 5, 1985.*

plate

4

Mary Shanahan *Art Director*
Lisa Atkin *Picture Editor*
Gentlemen's Quarterly, *Publication*
Condé Nast Publications Inc. *Publisher*

*Calvin Thompkins' book "Living Well is the Best Revenge" and memorabilia on Gerald
and Sara Murphy inspired the fashion feature "The Riviera Story." April 1986.*

Matt Mahurin

plate
5

Fabian Baron *Art Director*
New York Woman *Publication*
Esquire Magazine Group, Inc. *Publisher*

*"Dream Scapes," a lingerie feature, used three Matt Mahurin photos that emphasized
the sensuousness of silk and lace. September 1986.*

plate
6

plate
7

Nancy Butkus *Art Director*
Jane Clark *Picture Editor*
Manhattan, inc. *Publication*
Joyce Wadler *Writer*
Metrocorp *Publisher*

Larry Fink documented a day in Davir, an East Side beauty salon frequented
by the 'creme de la creme,' focusing on hairdresser "Sebou the Imperial," for
"Permanent Wave by Joyce Wadler. September 1986.

plate
8

plate
9

plate
10

plate
11

Herb Ritts

plate

12

Herb Ritts *Art Director*
Michael Roberts *Picture Editor*
Tatler Magazine *Publication*
Condé Nast Publications Inc. *Publisher*

Herb Ritts' photograph ran in a fashion spread featuring swimwear. April 1986.

Charles Reich

plate
13

Deb Hardison *Art Director*
Connecticut's Finest *Publication*
Charles Monagan *Writer*
Whittle Communications *Publisher*

*Charles Reich's series on Hartford includes details of a sculpture called "Winged Victory"
as part of his photo essay "The Indelible Images of Charles Reich." Spring 1986.*

plate
14

Fred Woodward *Art Director*
Texas Monthly *Publication*
Texas Monthly Inc. *Publisher*

These photographs appeared in a fashion article titled "Shadows in the Garden."

Fred Woodward

plate
15

plate
16

plate
17

plate
18

plate
19

plate
20

plate
21

Hans Neleman

plate
22

John Tennant *Art Director*
Collin Jacobsen *Picture Editor*
The Observer (London) *Publication*
London Observer *Publisher*

*Hans Neleman was given a free hand to "style, prop, conceptualize and execute the
setups" for a 12-part series on food. 1986.*

plate
23

plate
24

plate
25

plate
26

Robert J. Post *Art Director*
Chicago Magazine *Publication*
Christopher Lyon *Writer*
Metropolitan Communications Inc. *Publisher*

"A Woman of Fiber" is Christopher Lyon's study of art collector Claire Zeisler.
Victor Skrebneski's portrait accompanied Zeisler's exhibition at the Whitney in 1983.
November 1985.

plate
27

Robert J. Post *Art Director*
Chicago Magazine *Publication*
Alex Kotlowitz *Writer*
Metropolitan Communications Inc. *Publisher*

*Stephen Shames and Alex Kotlowitz's "Children of Poverty" draws attention to the
alarming rise in the number of needy children in Chicago. October 1985.*

plate
28

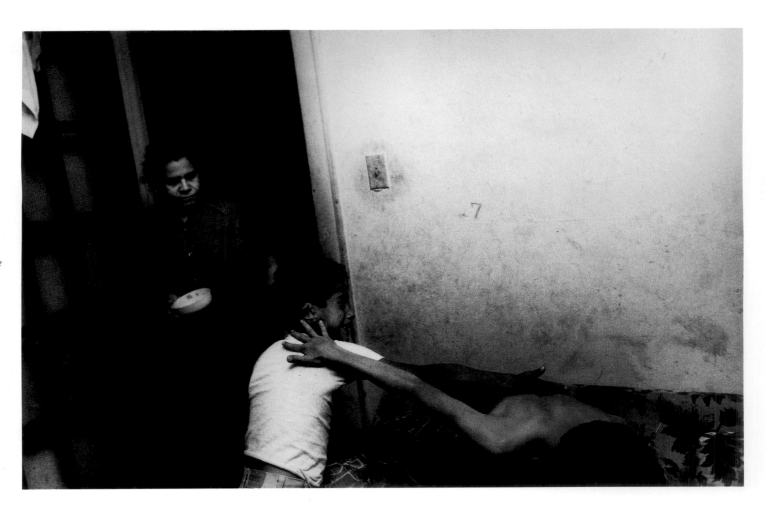

plate
29

plate

30

plate
31

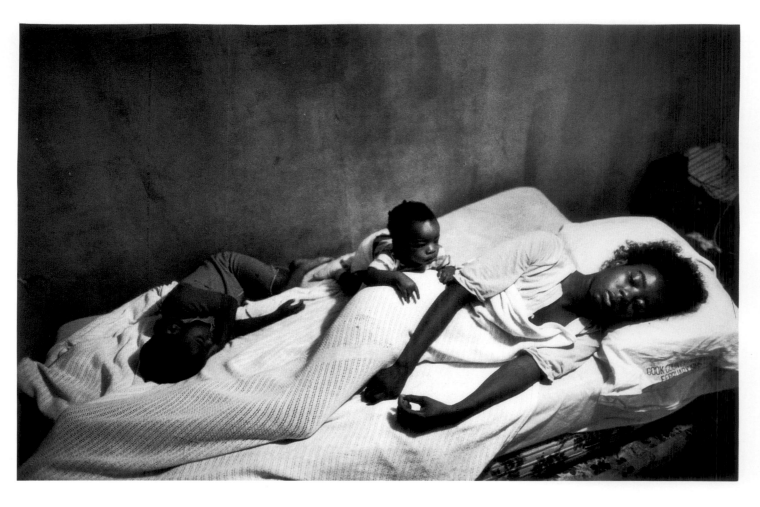

plate
32

Stephen Shames

plate
33

plate
34

Stephen Shames

plate
35

plate
36

plate
37

plate
38

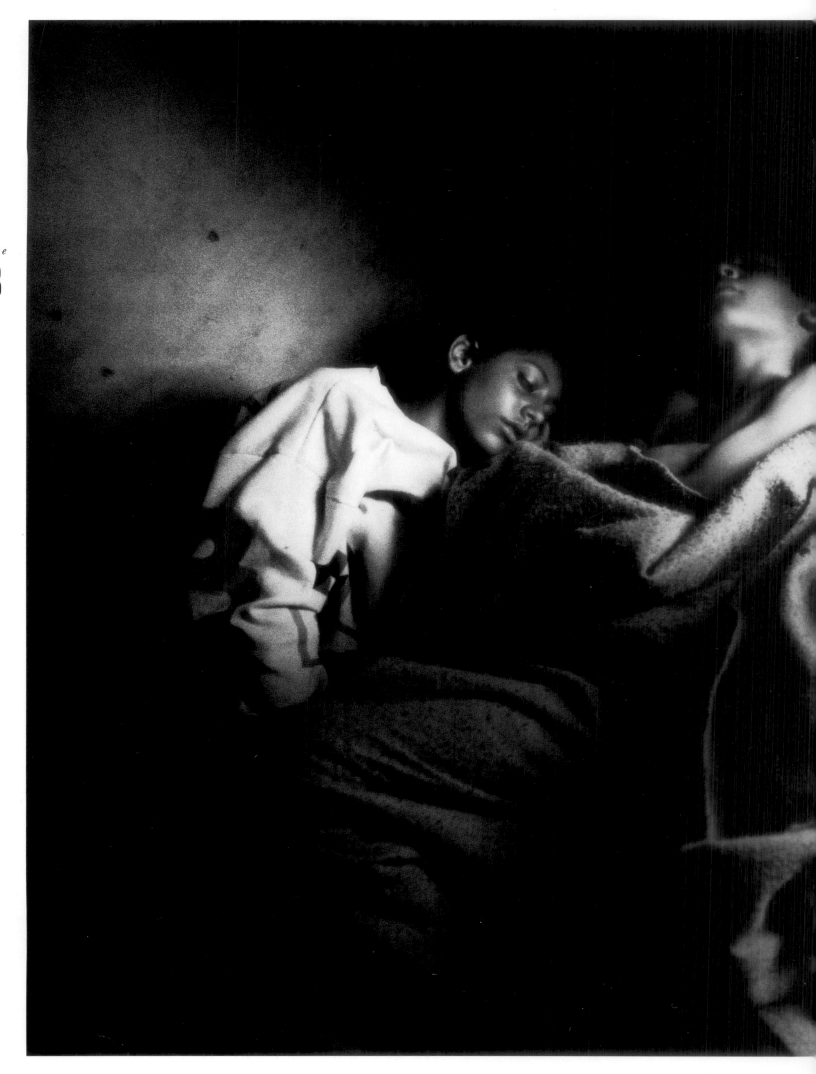

plate
39

Sheila Metzner

A series of shots for Jesse Kornbluth's "Journey Through Space: Christophe de Menil's
Search for a Uniquely Personal Environment." February 1986.

plate
40

Lloyd Ziff, Karen Lee Grant *Art Directors*
Thomas H. McWilliam, Jr. *Picture Editor*
House & Garden *Publication*
Jesse Kornbluth *Writer*
Condé Nast Publications Inc. *Publisher*

plate
41

Sheila Metzner

plate
42

Sheila Metzner

plate
43

Arthur Elgort

plate
44

Arthur Elgort

plate
45

Mary Shanahan *Art Director*
Lisa Atkin *Picture Editor*
Gentlemen's Quarterly *Publication*
Condé Nast Publications Inc. *Publisher*

*Extracts from Irwin Shaw's short story "The Girls in their Summer Dresses," for a
feature on summer clothes in New York City. July 1986.*

plate
46

plate
47

plate
48

plate
49

Derek Ungless *Art Director*
Laurie Kratochvil *Picture Editor*
Rolling Stone *Publication*
David Fricke *Writer*
Straight Arrow Publishers Inc. *Publisher*

*Matt Mahurin's study of singer Lou Reed for David Fricke's article
"Out of the Darkness." September 25, 1986.*

Matt Mahurin

plate
50

plate
51

Michael Rand *Art Director*
Gunn Brinson *Picture Editor*
The Sunday Times Magazine (London) *Publication*
Simon Winchester *Writer*
Times Newspapers Ltd. *Publisher*

*Mary Ellen Mark's photographs for Simon Winchester's "The Fuhrer's Ghost"
brought out the chilling aspects of the 1986 Aryan Nations Congress.
September 14, 1986.*

Mary Ellen Mark

plate
52

plate
53

plate
54

plate
55

plate
56

plate
57

Mary Shanahan *Art Director*
Lisa Atkin *Picture Editor*
Gentlemen's Quarterly *Publication*
Edward Kiersh *Writer*
Condé Nast Publications Inc. *Publisher*

*Alen Macweeney, author of "Irish Walls," recorded father and son's annual ritual of
shaving their heads for Edward Kiersh's article "The Prodigy." September 1986.*

Angel Franco

plate
58

Roger Black *Art Director*
Karen Mullarkey, Guy Cooper *Picture Editors*
Newsweek *Publication*
Newsweek, Inc. *Publisher*

Angel Franco visited several areas of New York City notorious for prevalent cocaine use
for Newsweek's special report on crack. June 16, 1986.

plate
59

plate
60

Matt Mahurin

plate
61

Jann Alexander *Art Director*
The Washington Post Magazine *Publication*
John Ed Bradley *Writer*
The Washington Post *Publisher*

*Entertainers and drugs, destroyed lives and death: Matt Mahurin's portrait
accompanied John Ed Bradley's cover story, "Murder, Drugs and the Rap Star."
September 7, 1986.*

Michael Geiger

plate
62

Derek Ungless *Art Director*
Laurie Kratochvil *Picture Editor*
Rolling Stone *Publication*
Richard Ford *Writer*
Straight Arrow Publishers Inc. *Publisher*

*Michael Geiger's closeup illustrated Richard Ford's "A Night in the Bushes," a
narrative about the "major pleasures offered the true baseball believer by a minor-league
game." September 25, 1986.*

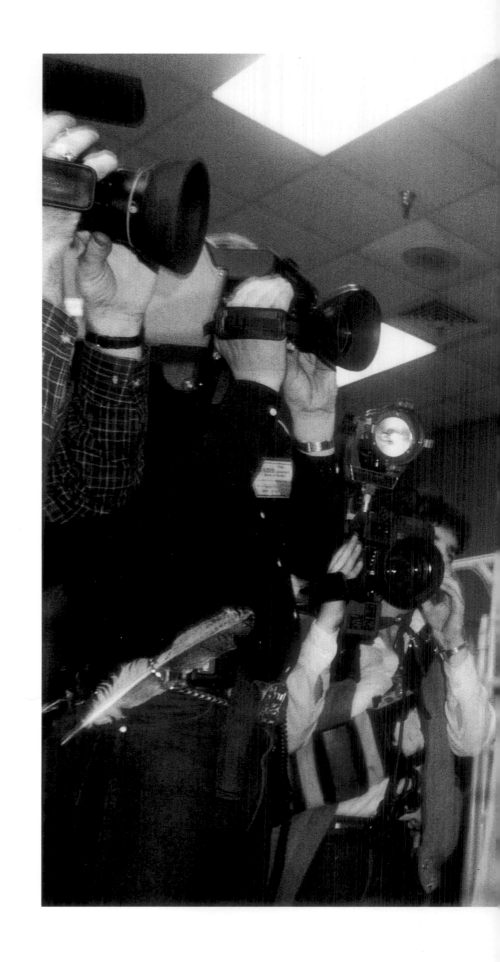

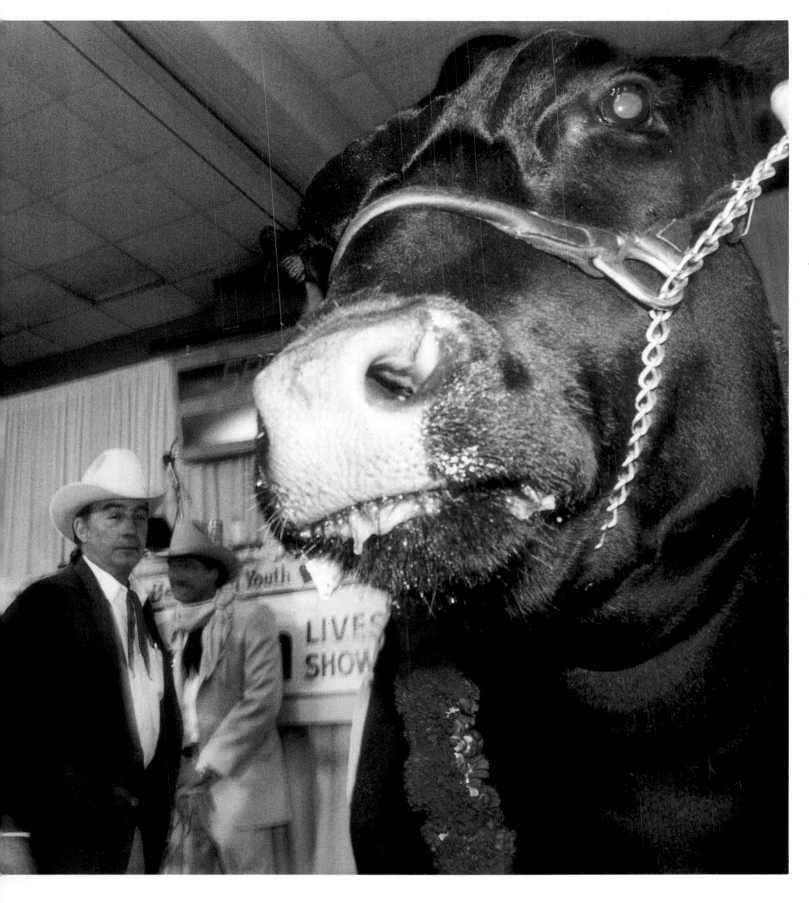

plate
63

Fred Woodward *Art Director*
Texas Monthly *Publication*
Texas Monthly, Inc. *Publisher*

*Geoff Winningham's photograph of the Grand Championship Steer Auction at the
Houston Livestock Show, which originally appeared in his book "A Place of Dreams:
Houston, An American City." September 1986.*

plate
64

Fred Woodward *Art Director*
Texas Monthly *Publication*
David Kramer *Writer*
Texas Monthly, Inc. *Publisher*

*David Kramer's article "Moments of Glory" featured these Texan Congressional
Medal of Honor winners. November 1986.*

Brian Smale

plate
65

plate
66

plate
67

Brian Smale

plate
68

Brian Smale

plate
69

plate
70

plate
71

Fred Woodward *Art Director*
Texas Monthly *Publication*
Aaron Latham *Writer*
Texas Monthly, Inc. *Publisher*

*Brian Smale sought out the men whose lives had inspired the movie "Urban Cowboy" and
photographed them for Latham's "The Return of the Urban Cowboy."*

plate
72

Benno Friedman

plate
73

Sally Ham *Art Director*
Campus Voice Weekly *Publication*
George Thomas *Writer*
Whittle Communications *Publisher*

Benno Friedman's portrait for George Thomas' article "Emo Philips: Nerd God."
January 1986.

Geof Kern

plate
74

Deborah Flynn-Hanrahan *Picture Editor*
Lotus Magazine *Publication*
Richard Cranford *Writer*
Lotus Publishing Corporation *Publisher*

Geof Kern was asked to illustrate an article on computers called "Distilling Data:
Advanced Uses for CD Functions." October 1986.

William Thompson

plate
75

Caroline Despard *Picture Editor*
Smithsonian Magazine *Publication*
Smithsonian Institution *Publisher*

*William Thompson was asked to "illuminate" the plight of the endangered
Southeast Asian rhinoceros while on a journey through Nepal.*

Sheila Metzner

plate
76

Franca Sozzani *Art Director*
Rosalie Glauser *Picture Editor*
Italia Vogue Bambini *Publication*
Edizioni Condé Nast S.P.A. *Publisher*

*"It was an intimate, romantic study of my daughter," Sheila Metzner says of her
assignment for Italia Vogue Bambini's "Fiorellini" feature. March/April 1986.*

plate

77

plate
78

plate
79

plate
80

Nancy Butkus *Art Director*
Jane Clark *Picture Editor*
Manhattan, inc. *Publication*
David Remnick *Writer*
Metrocorp *Publisher*

*Milton Petrie and his wife were photographed in their Fifth Avenue apartment for
David Remnick's "The Artful Codger." June 1986.*

Deborah Feingold

plate
81

Derek Ungless *Art Director*
Laurie Kratochvil *Picture Editor*
Rolling Stone *Publication*
Lewis Grossberger *Writer*
Straight Arrow Publishers Inc. *Publisher*

Deborah Feingold captures Rodney Dangerfield, the comedian who "gets no respect,"
in an introspective mood for Lewis Grossberger's "Respect At Last." August 28, 1986.

plate
82

Derek Ungless *Art Director*
Laurie Kratochvil *Picture Editor*
Rolling Stone *Publication*
Fred Schruers *Writer*
Straight Arrow Publishers Inc. *Publisher*

Jack Nicholson's grin shines through in Herb Ritts' underwater picture for
Fred Schruers' interview piece. August 14, 1986.

plate
83

Nancy Butkus *Art Director*
Jane Clark *Picture Editor*
Manhattan, inc. *Publication*
David Remnick *Writer*
Metrocorp *Publisher*

William Coupon's portrait of Milton Petrie for David Remnick's "Man's Best Friend."
June 1986.

George Lange

Nancy Butkus *Art Director*
Manhattan, inc. *Publication*
Ron Rosenbaum *Writer*
Metrocorp *Publisher*

Donald Trump is transformed into a pacifist during lunch at the "21" Club for
Ron Rosenbaum's "Trump: The Ultimate Deal." November 1985.

plate
84

George Lange

plate
85

plate
86

Bruce Ramsay *Art Director*
Saturday Night *Publication*
Keith Davey *Writer*
Saturday Night Group *Publisher*

One of Bernard Bohn's 'portraits environmentaux,' illustrating "The Sad Summer of '84," featured the Liberal Party's chief strategist, Sen. Keith Davey. October 1986.

plate

87

Advertising
and
Posters

Work for advertising in

consumer, trade and professional

periodicals and brochures,

as well as posters

Annie Leibovitz

plate
88

Lloyd Ziff *Art Director*
Executive Organizing Committee for the Mexico World Cup
Soccer Tournament, 1986 *Client*

*Annie Leibovitz was invited by the organizers of the 1986 World Cup
Soccer Tournament to go to Mexico and prepare a series of 13 posters showing
some of the participants. 1986.*

Annie Leibovitz

plate
89

plate
90

Annie Leibovitz

plate
91

Annie Leibovitz

plate
92

plate
93

plate
94

Annie Leibovitz

plate
95

plate
96

Jeff Ayeroff, Jeri McManus, Herb Ritts *Art Directors*
Madonna "True Blue" album cover *Publication*
Warner Brother Records *Client*

Herb Ritts' portrait of popular singer Madonna was used for the cover of the
"True Blue" record album. Fall 1986.

Dennis Manarchy

plate
97

Rick Boyko *Art Director*
Bill Hamilton *Copywriter*
Nike *Client*
Chiat/Day, Inc. *Agency*

*Ease and comfort were emphasized in this photo by Dennis Manarchy for a
Nike Runningwear advertisement. Spring 1986.*

plate
98

Rick Boyko *Art Director*
Bill Hamilton *Copywriter*
Nike *Client*
Chiat/Day, Inc. *Agency*

*Dennis Manarchy's photo for Nike Fitnesswear was used in an advertisement showing
fashion-conscious women participating in sports. Fall 1986.*

Promotion

*All forms of design
photographs including technical
or industrial literature,
brochures, annual reports,
calendars and self-
promotion pieces*

plate
99

Jeff Ayeroff *Art Director*
Jeri McManus *Designer*
Warner Brothers Records *Client*

*The record "Tenku" (which translates roughly as "infinite expansion") featured
Matt Mahurin's portrait of the musician Kitaro on its cover.*

Charles Ford

plate
100

Joan Ford *Designer*

The photo shown is from a series of self-promotional cards distributed by Charles Ford.

plate
101

Judith Henry *Designer*
Laurie Silbersweig *Editor*
Harry N. Abrams, Inc. *Publisher*

Tokyo-born Toshi Otsuki's photographs appear in the 1987 Central Park Calendar.

Toshi Otsuki

plate
102

plate
103

Toshi Otsuki

plate
104

plate
105

Kevin Kuester *Art Director*
Madsen & Kuester, Inc. *Design Group*
Wells & Company *Writer*
Potlatch Corporation *Publisher*

*These two photographs appeared in a brochure promoting a type of paper
called Eloquence Gloss.*

plate
106

Jim Rantala

plate
107

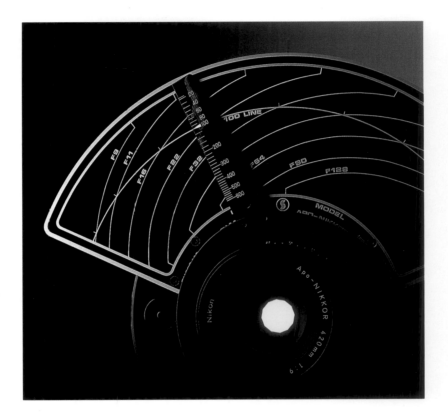

Bill Gramley *Art Director*
Rob Pawlak *Designer*
The CPS Group *Designer Group*
Les Gibson *Writer*

From a series of photos representing services offered by the CPS Group, by Jim Rantala.

Jim Rantala

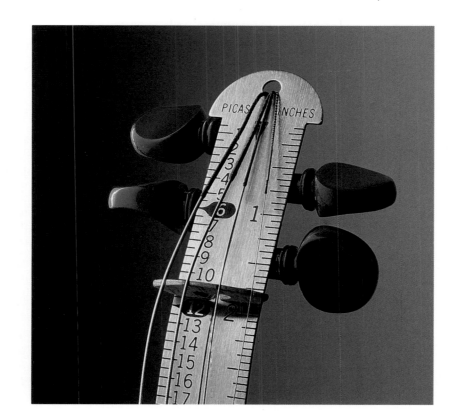

plate
108

Jim Rantala

plate
109

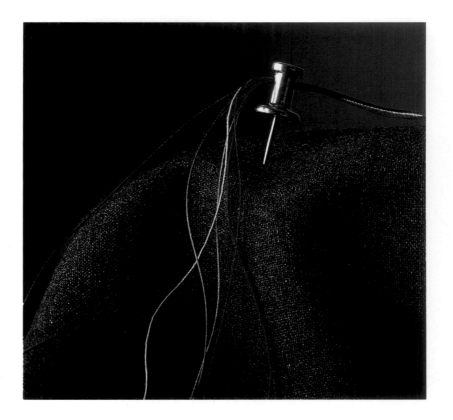

Jim Rantala

plate
110

plate
111

*"Fluorescent Lady" appeared in mailers sent out by Ralph Cowan, whose work includes
studies with ultraviolet lights.*

plate
112

Cheryl Heller *Designer*
HBM/Creamer *Design Group*

*Clint Clemens found outrageous cars and locations for S. D. Warren Paper's
"Hot Rods in California."*

Duane Michals

plate
113

Christopher Austopchuk *Art Director*
CBS Records *Design Group*

Duane Michals created images of musicians for the record album cover "Smash Palace."

plate
114

plate
115

plate
116

Books

Photographs for non-fiction books

plate
117

Lloyd Ziff *Designer*
James Danziger *Editor*
Visual Aid *Title*
Pantheon *Publisher*

*"Visual Aid," inspired by the musicians who participated in Band Aid and
U.S.A. for Africa, was shot by Matthew Rolston, Herb Ritts, Greg Gorman,
Annie Leibovitz and others. 1986.*

plate
118

plate
119

plate
120

plate
121

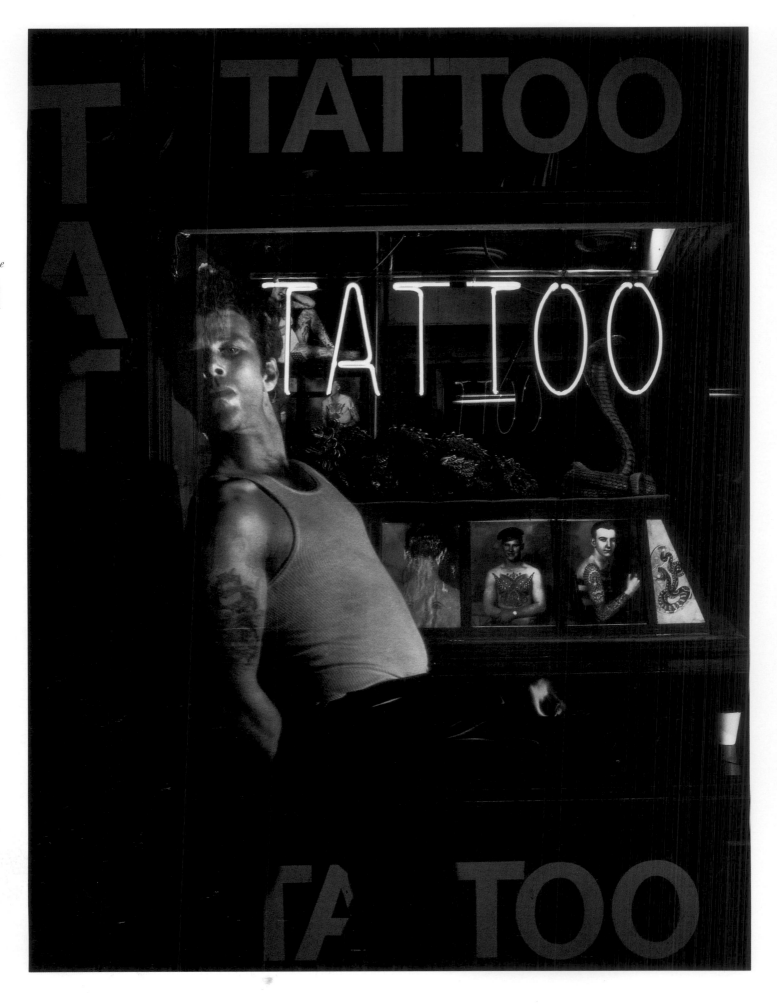

Annie Leibovitz

plate
122

plate
123

plate
124

Kurt Markus

plate
125

Jack Woody *Designer*
After Barbed Wire: Cowboys of Our Time *Title*
Twelvetrees Press *Publisher*

*Kurt Markus' many studies of ranch life in the American West evolved into the
December 1985 book.*

Kurt Markus

plate
126

plate
127

Kurt Markus

plate

128

plate
129

Joel-Peter Witkin *Title*
Twelvetrees Press *Publisher*

Joel-Peter Witkin includes in his monograph "All manner of visual perversions…
any living myth." Shown here are "Woman Breastfeeding an Eel, New Mexico, 1979"
and "Harvest, Philadelphia, 1984."

plate
130

Alice Springs

plate
131

Jack Woody *Editor*
Alice Springs: Portraits *Title*
Twelvetrees Press *Publisher*

"Alice Springs' Portraits," with an introduction by Helmut Newton, were taken over
a 10-year period. October 1986.

plate
132

Alice Springs

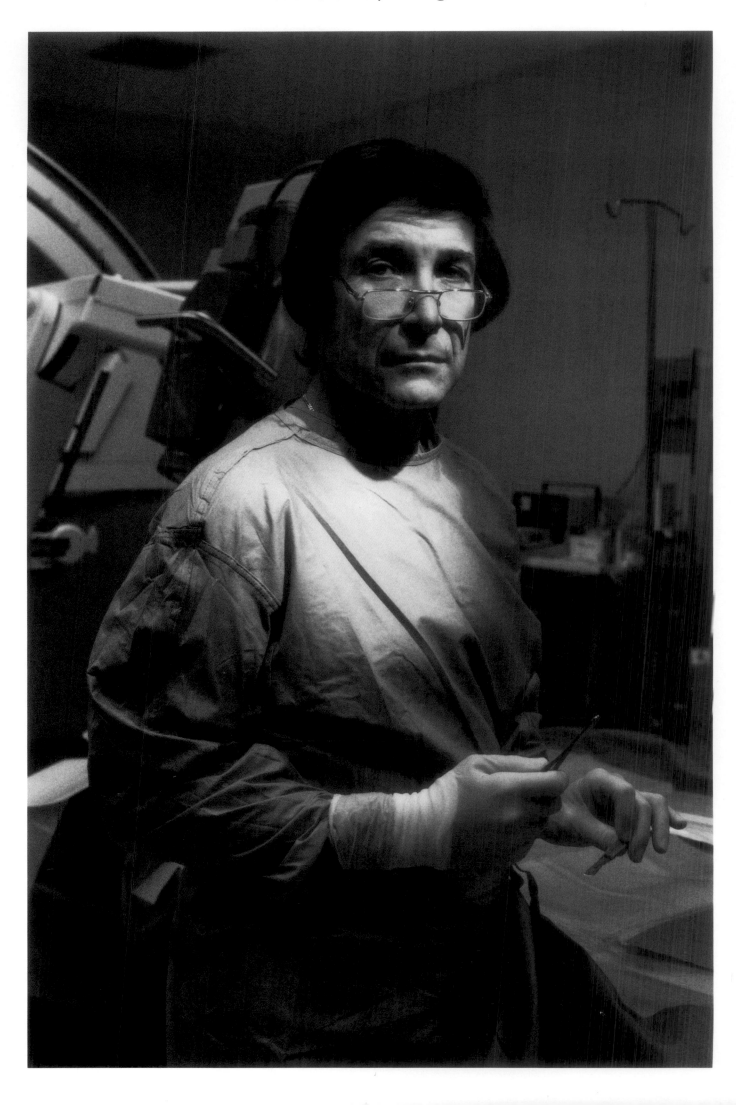

plate
133

plate
134

plate
135

plate
136

Jack Shear

plate
137

Jack Woody *Designer*
Four Marines and Other Portraits *Title*
Twelvetrees Press *Publisher*

Portraits of author William Burroughs and Vito Banoza, from Jack Shear's monograph
"Four Marines and Other Portraits." December 1985.

Jack Shear

plate
138

Duane Michals

plate
139

Jack Woody *Designer*
The Nature of Desire *Title*
Twelvetrees Press *Publisher*

"I must write this now, this very moment," begins Duane Michals in "The Nature of Desire," a compilation of his poems and photographs. October 1986.

plate
140

plate
141

Duane Michals

plate
142

plate
143

Tyler Smith *Designer*
Out of Mexico *Title*
Universal Press *Publisher*

*Clint Clemens and Tyler Smith drove through Mexico in a bus loaded with sculpture
to get shots for "Out of Mexico," a book on Mexican artist Sergio Bustamante.
January 1987.*

plate
144

plate
145

Sheila Metzner

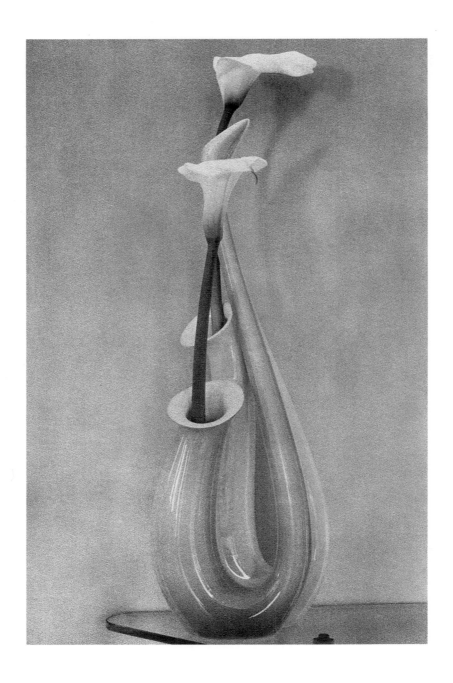

Katy Homans *Designer*
Constance Sullivan *Editor*
Objects of Desire *Title*
Clarkson N. Potter, Inc. *Publisher*

*"Objects of Desire," published in 1986, looks at an evolution in style that covers about
10 years. Shown here are "The Saxophone Vase," "Stella Galaxy," "Bega Peppers"
and "Borneo Girl"*

plate
147

I SERVED TIME IN PRISON: A Woman's Poignant Confession

plate
148

Unpublished Work

*Commissioned but
unpublished photographs,
and personal work by
professionals, amateurs
and students*

plate
149

*Philadelphia, New Year's Day: Burk Uzzle took these double portraits
two months apart—the mummers in costume and at home.*

plate
150

plate
151

Ethel Wolvovitz, a kindergarten teacher, takes pictures in her school every Halloween.
She caught the formidable "Dean of Discipline" between classes.

Yuri Dojc

plate
152

*Yuri Dojc was in the Bahamas when he photographed "Double Dolphin" using
a model and toy dolphins.*

plate
153

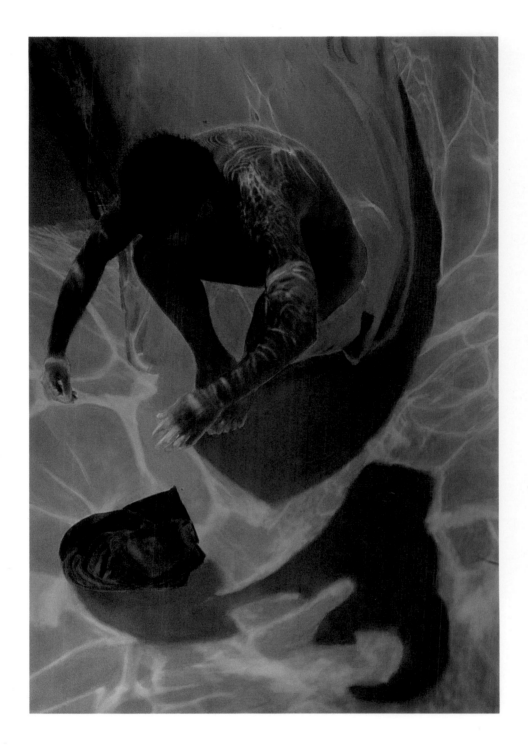

Curtis Taylor did this handpainted photograph in the summer of 1986.

plate
154

A pair of eyeglasses, a comb and tweezers drawn together for Charles Purvis' "Untitled 2."

Orah Moore

plate
155

*Orah Moore shot "Reins" as part of her Montana Ranch series when she
returned to this remote area "intent on learning more about a lifestyle I only vaguely
thought still existed."*

Harvey Butts

plate
156

Harvey Butts has led a continuous search for abandoned cars throughout New York City.
Shown here are "George Washington Bridge from Riverside Park," "Mustang on the
West Side Highway," "The Harlem River Drive," and "Long Island City # 2."

Harvey Butts

plate
157

plate
158

plate
159

plate
160

Barbara Kasten's "Architectural Site 6, July 14, 1986" and "Architectural Site 7,
July 14, 1986" were originally commissioned by Vanity Fair. These shots were taken at
New York's World Trade Center.

Barbara Kasten

plate
161

plate
162

*"Nevada Sex Ranch" is Timothy Hursley's document of the brothels that proliferated
in the state that legalized prostitution.*

plate
163

plate
164

Timothy Hursley

plate
165

plate
166

plate
167

Index

*Names and addresses
of photographers.
Index of picture editors,
editors, designers, art
directors, writers,
publications, publishers,
design groups,
advertising agencies
and clients*

PHOTOGRAPHERS

Jonathan Becker
450 West 24th Street
New York, NY 10011
Plate 80

Bernard Bohn
4060 St. Laurent
Suite 409
Montreal, Quebec H2W 1V9
Canada
Plate 87

Harvey Butts
25 Cambridge Place
Brooklyn, NY 11238
Plates 156, 157, 158, 159

Chris Callis
91 Fifth Avenue
Brooklyn, NY 10003
Plate 3

Clint Clemens
346 Newbury Street
Boston, MA 02115
Plates 112, 143, 144

William Coupon
237 Lafayette Street
11th Floor
New York, NY 10012
Plate 83

Ralph Cowan
452 North Halsted Street
Chicago, IL 60622
Plate 111

Yuri Dojc
632 Briar Hill Avenue
Toronto, Ontario M5N 1N2
Canada
Plate 152

Arthur Elgort
136 Grand Street
New York, NY 10003
Plates 44, 45, 46, 47, 48, 49

Deborah Feingold
151 West 19th Street
New York, NY 10011
Plate 81

Larry Fink
Box 295
Martins Creek, PA 18063
Plates 8, 9, 10, 11

Charles Ford
32 East 22nd Street
New York, NY 10010
Plate 100

Angel Franco
145 West 105th Street 4E
New York, NY 10025
Plates 58, 59, 60

Benno Friedman
26 West 20th Street
New York, NY 10011
Plate 73

Michael Geiger
Post Office Box 946
Tillson, NY 12486
Plate 62

Greg Gorman
1351 Miller Drive
Los Angeles, CA 90069
Plates 119, 121

Pamela Hanson
c/o Oversee, Inc.
153 Mercer Street
New York, NY 10012
Plate 4

George Hurrell
6702 St. Clair Avenue
North Hollywood, CA 91606
Plates 1, 2

Timothy Hursley
1911 West Markham
Little Rock, AR 72205
Plates 162, 163, 164, 165,
166, 167

Barbara Kasten
38 West 26th Street
New York, NY 10010
Plates 160, 161

Geof Kern
1337 Crampton
Dallas, TX 75207
Plate 74

George Lange
817 West End Avenue # 7A
New York, NY 10025
Plates 84, 85, 86

Annie Leibovitz
101 West 18th Street
New York, NY 10011
Plates 88, 89, 90, 91, 92
93, 94, 95, 122, 123

Alen MacWeeney
171 First Avenue
New York, NY 10013
Plate 57

Matt Mahurin
77 Bleecker Street # 102
New York, NY 10012
Plates 5, 6, 7, 50, 61, 99

Dennis Manarchy
229 West Illinois
Chicago, IL 60610
Plates 97, 98

Mary Ellen Mark
143 Prince Street
Third Floor
New York, NY 10012
Plates 51, 52, 53, 54, 55, 56

Kurt Markus
9555 Bennision
Colorado Springs, CO 80908
Plates 124, 125, 126, 127, 128

Sheila Metzner
310 Riverside Drive
New York, NY 10025
Plates 39, 40, 41, 42, 43, 76
77, 78, 79, 145, 146, 147, 148

Arthur Meyerson
4215 Bellaire Boulevard
Houston, TX 77025
Plates 105, 106

Duane Michals
109 East 19th Street
New York, NY 10003
Plates 113, 114, 115, 116, 139
140, 141, 142

Orah Moore
1691 Oakdale Street # B
Pasadena, CA 91106
Plate 155

Hans Neleman
c/o Wheeler Pictures
145 West 28th Street
New York, NY 10001
Plates 22, 23, 24, 25

Tosh Otsuki
241 West 36th Street
6th Floor
New York, NY 10018
Plates 101, 102, 103, 104

Charles Purvis
84 Thomas Street, # 3
New York, NY 10013
Plate 154

Jim Rantala
932 Allston
Houston, TX 77008
Plates 107, 108, 109, 110

Charles Reich
56 Arbor Street
Hartford, CT 06106
Plate 13

Herb Ritts
7927 Hillside Avenue
Los Angeles, CA 90046
Plates 12, 82, 96, 120

Matthew Rolston
8259 Melrose Avenue
Hollywood, CA 90046
Plates 117, 118

Steven Shames
c/o Visions, Inc.
105 Fifth Avenue
New York, NY 10003
Plates 27, 28, 29, 30, 31, 32
33, 34, 35, 36, 37, 38

Jack Shear
Box 151
Spencertown, NY 12165
Plates 137, 138

Victor Skrebneski
1350 North LaSalle
Chicago, IL 60610
Plate 26

Brian Smale
230 Ontario Street
Toronto, Ontario M5A 2V5
Canada
Plates 64, 65, 66, 67, 68, 69,
70, 71, 72

Alice Springs
c/o Twelvetrees Press
Post Office Box 188
Pasadena, CA 91102
Plates 131, 132, 133, 134
135, 136

Curtice Taylor
29 East 22nd Street
New York, NY 10010
Plate 153

William Thompson
Post Office Box 4460
Seattle, WA 98104
Plate 75

Burk Uzzle
737 North Fourth Street
Philadelphia, PA 19123
Plates 149, 150

Geoff Winningham
2020 Wroxton
Houston, TX 77005
Plate 63

Joel Peter-Witkin
c/o Twelvetrees Press
Post Office Box 188
Pasadena, CA 91102
Plates 129, 130

Ethel Wolvovitz
305 Ocean Parkway
Brooklyn, NY 11218
Plate 151

Fred Woodward
2 Swift Alley
Alexandria, VA 22314
Plates 14, 15, 16, 17, 18,
19, 20, 21

Edward Booth-Clibborn, *President*
Donna Vinciguerra, *Project Director*

THE COMMITTEE

Bob Ciano, *Art Director,* Life *magazine, New York*
B. Martin Pedersen, *Designer, Jonson, Pirtle, Pedersen, Alcorn, Metzdorf, and Hess, New York*
Robert Priest, *Art Director,* US *magazine, New York*
Derek W. Ungless, *Art Director,* Rolling Stone *magazine, New York*

American Photography, Inc., 67 Irving Place, New York, New York 10003   (212) 460-5558